Guide and Hack WiFi

Content

What WiFi networks mean 5
Is it legal to hack into a WiFi network? 5
Types of WiFi network security to hack into 8
How to check the security of a WiFi network 9
The most used characters on WiFi network passwords 13
Factors that compromise a WiFi network 15
Tricks to decrypt WiFi network keys for Linux 19
How to hack a WiFi network from Linux without graphics card 24
What you need to know to hack WiFi from Android 26
Discover how to hack WPA and WPA2 networks without using a dictionary 32
Hacking WiFi networks with PMKID 36
How to obtain WiFi network keys with BlackTrack 5 37
The secrets to hack WiFi networks without programs 39
Acrylic, WEP and WPA WiFi Network Hacking 42
Rainbow tables as a password cracking technique 44
Get to know the KRACK tool for hacking WiFi networks 45
Hacking WiFi networks using Wifimosys 50
Jumpstart for hacking WiFi networks from Windows 52
How to decrypt the WiFi key on a Mac 54
Advanced tools for auditing WiFi networks 57
Decrypt WiFi passwords stored on the cell phone 59
Alternatives to hack WiFi networks 65
How to decrypt WiFi network passwords according to companies 70
The best way to hack WiFi networks, step by step 77
Kali Linux: the most effective hacking of networks 81
Learn how to decrypt WiFi networks with Aircrack-ng 83

The fastest method to hack WiFi networks 85

How to break the router's default password 87

Faults available behind the routers 88

Tips and requirements for hacking WiFi networks 90

What to do when hacking methods are used on your WiFi networks 92

The maximum security of the WPA3 protocol 93

WiFi networks are not impenetrable, with the right tricks and procedures, you can have a connection without knowing the password, if you have always wanted to be connected without limitation, this is the best way to make it happen, taking into account the type of system from which it can be hacked.

The security of each router leaves a possibility, i.e. its security level is challenged with a factory defect, as they also possess a certain vulnerability to the various procedures that arise every day, because for each model of WiFi network, there is an opportunity to challenge the security of this kind of connection.

What WiFi networks mean

The WiFi is a mechanism that works wirelessly, it allows to open the way to internet access to different devices, it is a technology linked to different modoso of uses, where the absence of cables is established as a clear solution, that connection is carried out through the use of infrared.

The transmission of information is guaranteed, because one of the qualities of this technology is the immediacy, but the condition is that the user has a place over the range and capacity of WiFi networks, the normal radius is between 5 and 150 meters away from the emission of the signal.

The configuration is a key aspect in the topic of WiFi network hacking, it is very simple and when it is not covered there is a real headache, also the WiFi card of the devices has a lot to do so that the connection can be used at its maximum expression, so that the compatibility of the network is not affected.

Is it legal to hack into a WiFi network?

The wireless internet connection is what characterizes a WiFi network, this emission of information or data through waves creates the opportunity for many people to have access to it, which is not irrelevant information because one of its low points is security.

The dimension of a WiFi network and its expansion, causes it to be accessible in any type from anywhere with its coverage radius point, these are even without password due to lack of configuration of the administrators, which can reduce the speed of loading internet data, because third parties can connect to the network.

However, with the creation of the password, you are not safe either, because many methods allow you to attack that network and be part of it, which is classified as computer fraud, since you do not have the consent of the owner, and it reflects an extra charge on consumption and in some cases decreasing the speed of access.

That connection is interpreted as a patrimony of another person, therefore it is an illegal damage that type of use, especially because that unauthorized use is causing an increase of fee on the WiFi service provider, at the level of Europe, this type of actions have been included on the Penal Code.

The legal penalties for hacking WiFi networks, including imprisonment for a period exceeding three years, plus an economic amount to the affected party, this is the risk that is run at the time of hacking this kind of connection, also the measure of this crime is based on the methods used to carry out this action.

Normally the type of legal penalty that is applied is an amount of less than 400 euros, and a fine not exceeding three months, what can be measured or proven is the increase in internet consumption due to the existence of an additional connection that is not authorized, to reach this determination programs that manage network activity are used.

In the same way that programs are used to hack a connection, in the same way utilities have been designed to counteract the entry of unauthorized third parties, i.e. they are applications that protect the use of WiFi networks, even having the possibility of encrypting the network.

The most usual signs for users to think that their network is being hacked is the drop in speed, that kind of inconvenience is what causes a wake-up call, and programs that measure consumption, deliver daily reports or record it, that way they can start to have indications and evidence of the extra consumption of an intruder.

Types of WiFi network security to hack into

Each of the WiFi networks, has security standards, this is imposed as a barrier so that there is no unauthorized access, the most common to attack to gain access to the connection, are the following:

- **WEP**

It is part of a security protocol known as 802.11 standard, it was ratified since 1997, its acronym corresponds to: Wired Equivalent Privacy, it establishes a security algorithm that is obsolete on wireless networks, it takes care of confidentiality, but in the same way it is possible to hack in just a few minutes.

- **WPA**

It is the replacement of WEP, it is known as a stable security standard, it was released in 2003, its acronym is illustrated as Wi-Fi Protected Access, it is a prevention against the attacks suffered by WEP, its operation is based on temporary keys, it designates a key per packet, and it has message checking.

- **WPA2**

Its origin is anchored to the replacement of WPA, it has an implementation of more elements, up to a support and encryption, merging aspect of the previous ones to improve the level of response to attacks, so hacking this type of security, requires steps or executions that are more sophisticated.

This makes it easier to target WiFi networks that have WEP for example, since weakness is the first thing to exploit, to circumvent security standards that seek to perfect every flaw.

How to check the security of a WiFi network

An audit can be carried out on a WiFi network, to study and certify its security. Normally, software such as WiFi Auditor is used, which runs on Windows systems, has an advanced operation on computing, and is compatible with any computer with Java.

This new audit feature limits a little the margin of hacking that can occur on a WiFi network, especially because these softwares have extended their version for Mac OS X, this help leaves aside some level of vulnerability that presents the network, but in its operation of protection, it is also able to provide passwords.

- **WiFi Auditor as a hacking tool**

The power of WiFi Auditor provides information about the passwords of WiFi networks that are vulnerable, as well as those that do not have security, so it would be a tool that is useful to use these passwords to connect for free to the Internet for free.

The basic options of this software are very easy to understand, you just need to click on the "network audit" option for the program to carry out its functions, it is an automatic job that provides security vulnerability data that gives you control and power over those networks.

The detection of security weaknesses also has a lot to do with the router being used, because its level of vulnerability can cause the password to be obtained in a few seconds, impacting on the algorithms that have been made public taking into account the MAC address.

The type of passwords that can be countered by WiFiAuditor are those with the following characteristics or description:

- Those networks that by default keep the original name imposed by the router itself.
- Default passwords are usually the same as the one inserted on the back of the router.

- Networks that are close together, without obstacles or interferences such as large walls, allowing the transmitter and the use of the software to have full contact.
- The router has a public and identifiable algorithm.

This is due to the fact that the study or identification performed by this software is able to have access to the password or at least to the router, this kind of free way allows the internet connection to be provided by this tool.

WiFi Auditor vs. WiFislax features

A comparison between WiFislax and WiFi Auditor, which are widely used nowadays, due to the simplicity of their functions, causing the disclosure of WiFi passwords to be more common than usual, before comparing both, it is advisable to check the local legislation about the use of these softwares to avoid any problem.

The first differential point between one software and the other is that WiFislax is not compatible with Windows, but WiFi Auditor can work with this type of operating system, and it does not require any type of installation, it works with the most modern version of Windows, because it works as a JAVA virtual machine.

On the other hand, in terms of results, both alternatives are efficient to study any type of network that is nearby, although if you have a powerful antenna, the range is significantly increased, it is advisable to opt for a directional panel, being one of the best options to take advantage of both software.

- ## The WiFi Auditor installation process

One of the requirements to install WiFi Aditor is to have JAVA, which excludes any type of use on Android, but if it is available with Windows and MAC Apple, its operation is fast and simple, unlike WiFislax that has more advanced options and requires more time, but only supports Linux.

The execution of these softwares allows to carry out two alternatives, firstly the audit networks, and connect, in that way you can generate the decryption of key that is possible, this is issued directly on the screen, and drives the connection, its application is simple without any manual is put in place.

The best thing about this type of software is that it is not classified as illegal, it is a mathematical calculation, so as such it does not crack passwords or is not designed to do so, but its operations expose the router models' own flaws, making it easy to guess the type of key it has.

The internet providers themselves, are what expose online the type of password they have by default, and when the administrator does not make a change on them, is that this gap of opportunity to hack the network is presented, what is illegal is the use of that WiFi network without consent, but the lawful obtaining is another aspect.

The WiFi Auditor program does not provide passwords that have been customized by the user, this type of change is not easy to detect, nor is it compatible with the functions of the software, its action is on vulnerable networks and user carelessness, the brands with the greatest margin of weakness is Dlink, Axtel, Verizom, Tecom and others.

The most used characters on WiFi network passwords

The formation of a password in a WiFi network, when customized, complicates any kind of hacking attempt, however most users do not perform this step, but use this network under default values, the programs maintain a dictionary of the most possible ones, to breach the security of such a network.

The most commonly used values are numeric, Latin alphabet in lowercase or uppercase, alphanumeric, hexadecimal in both uppercase and lowercase, even special characters can be incorporated, factory-set passwords have a hexadecimal set of 16 possible character types.

This type of information or data, reduces the possibility in great proportions, leaving that the algorithm is in charge of discarding the compatibilities with the password, for that reason it is a lack of security to leave the key that is imposed in a predetermined way, for that reason the recommended thing is that they place 12 characters.

On the other hand, when a key is inserted on the WiFi network, brute force must be implemented for a timely decryption, depending on the power or capacity of the computer, otherwise the time to discover the key increases proportionally, usually the keys that have a length of 8 digits take from 7 to 93 days.

When variables such as uppercase and lowercase are joined, the wait can be up to years, i.e. when dealing with more complex passwords, even the best program will not be able to act effectively, as each one develops mathematical operations, in the middle of the cracking process.

Faced with this negative scenario of complex passwords, the only way to speed this up is with a correct implementation of equipment, where the graphics card stands out, this must be powerful, so that it has a performance of 350,000 WPA or WPA2 hashes per second, since this means that it studies up to 350,000 passwords.

When FPGA-sized hardwares are incorporated, a performance of up to 1,750,000 hashes per second is presented, being a considerable difference, this is essential to know beforehand, since if the password is not long, and it is not found on the dictionary, it means that it is a long delayed process.

Factors that can compromise a WiFi network

Finding the vulnerability of a WiFi network completely compromises all levels of security. This fatal result can occur when different factors concur, i.e. the following scenarios can lead to malicious acts:

1. DNS Hijacking

A network can receive an attack from Internet browsing, because the Domain Name System (DNS) allows communication between a device and the network, that kind of function can be mastered by a cracker, to change the DNS of the real provider, in exchange for his own, as a malicious decoy.

When this type of change occurs, the user can open a portal, and will not be sure it is the correct one, but may be on a site controlled by the attacker, but retains the appearance of the original website, this is unnoticeable by the user, but when you enter your information, it will be sent to the attacker.

This type of risk has more to do with the security of personal data, as it is also a process implemented by WiFi network hacking programs, in some cases the browser itself issues a communication, or some warning signal to users to let them know that something is wrong.

2. Botnets

This factor reveals that some routers have remote access, many are turned on under a default mode, this creates an opportunity to enter the router through that remote path, this happens through the use of Secure Shell server known as SHH, as well as a Telnet server or with a web interface is carried out.

When a user does not change these default passwords, direct access services are allowed to connect through the Internet, leaving aside any type of protection, since anyone can have access, since they would only have to use a program to detect the default data, which is simple.

In addition, this type of data is published on the Internet, causing computer attacks to be more effective, these types of situations or characteristics are exposed and leave security unanswered.

3. Traffic monitoring

Currently, spying tools are being developed, one of them that directly affects a WiFi network is traffic monitoring, one of the most popular is tcpdump, which is directly associated with the router, to collect all encrypted communication that is transmitted through the router.

4. Proxy

The invisibility of the attackers is another factor that directly affects WiFi networks, in this maneuver the attackers do not perform any type of installation, since they only need the SSH to be available, thus it is adopted as a disguise, an invisible address is created, and before any attack their address is not exposed but the one that has been breached.

5. Vulnerable protocols

Different protocols such as UPnP, Bonjour, Zeroconf, and SSDP, provide an open path, this is tested by the applications that are part of the dynamics of the internet of things devices, and routers, and in the absence of updating these protocols, a notorious failure arises, being an opportunity for an attack.

To understand it better, it is necessary to process that a protocol such as Universal Plug and Play (UPnP), summarizes the configuration of PlayStation level equipment as well as Skpe, this kind of programs, opens the door to more users to be part of the development of its functions, and this causes the IP address to be public.

Any type of failure with the use of UPnP, directly on the router, causes flaws to come to light, and this allows more attackers to gain access to the internal network, so they are protocols that enable functions, but in turn, put everything at risk.

6. Weak passwords

The routers that are part of the WiFi, use different encryption mechanisms, it can be an open network, without any type of encryption, as well as the well-known WPA2, it is advisable not to apply methods that do not have guarantees such as WEP and WPA, because they are decrypted quite easily.

WPA2 personal encryption is one of the most reliable, but it all depends on the decision that can be made about the password, since one that has at least eight digits can be decrypted in a few minutes, especially when using brute force attack programs.

When a user does not take the WiFi network key seriously, problems arise, as it is an easy point for attackers to connect to the router, and this causes the devices connected to the network to be exposed as well, although attacks also target vulnerabilities in the router's firmware.

Tips for decrypting WiFi network keys for Linux

The interest in decrypting the key of third party WiFi networks is increasing, it is a task that above complex only requires knowledge, because with the right tips and extra preparation, you can have the ability to obtain any type of key, although the use of such data, are at your own legal risk.

When you want to hack a WiFi network, the procedure changes depending on the type of operating system from which this action will be carried out, so it is classified as follows:

- **Preparation for Linux**

In the case of hacking from a Linux system, you must have or incorporate the following:

1. **Aircrack-ng:** It represents a Suite of several programs, being useful to attack WiFi networks, this series of programs host packets to generate attacks, this type of programs are the ones that decrypt the keys, either WEP or WPA.
2. **USB network card:** This is an addition that can be PCI.
3. **Reaver-wps:** These are types of programs that take advantage of the failures on the WPA incorporation, thanks to the WPS.

Once these three requirements are obtained, it is time to audit the network to obtain the WiFi key, the main thing is to install Aircracck-ng, it has a 32-bit and 64-bit version, once installed, it is time to have the USB network card, such cards have more capacity than others, the one that stands out is RTL8187 chipset.

The stability of this type of card is attractive, and all the programs are able to work with it, you only have to link them, to go to the last step of downloading the reaver-wps, this is the one that helps to detect the vulnerabilities that exist, to apply blunt attacks against the WPS, and find the security pin.

The best way to get the WiFi network key, is to place the network device under a monitor mode, in addition to studying the possibility of applying packets on the WiFi network, then you can use the airmon-ng command, thus working on obtaining the key, the steps to follow are as follows:

1. **Execution of Iwconfig:** This function helps to detect the WiFi card, by observing that number you can carry out another command, which indicates the name of the device.
2. **Create the device to extract the key:** The creation of a device is what allows injecting on the network to be mastered, for this it is vital to enter the command "sudo airmon-ng start (device name)", to activate this option you must be root.
3. **Status check:** Information is provided on the screen, when entering the "iwconfig" command, indicating the activation of the monitor mode on the device, through which the WiFi key will be sought to be decrypted.

4. **Execution of the key breaking:** To measure the operation of the previous steps, it is only necessary to start the device, for that you must have aireplay-ng, this is provided by aircrack-ng, just run the command "aireplay-ng -test mono", this under the administrator mode.

The result of the above action, emits the result of "injection is working", so you can find out if the packet injection works, it is a way to crack the WiFi key, bringing out the vulnerabilities behind the network configuration.

Another simpler alternative to carry out this procedure through Linux, where it is vital to download Kali Linux, for being one of the most essential tools, the following is to have the USB memory to be a bootable drive, and in its memory will be the Kali Linux ISO file to install it later.

Investing in a WiFi card facilitates the whole procedure, it is a way to monitor all the information on the Wi-Fi network, after this point it is vital to log in as a root user, this is key to carry out the hacking process, that connection between the WiFi card to the computer is what sets the whole process in motion.

After these previous steps have been completed, the following steps must be executed:

- Open the terminal of the computer that has Kali Linux, the first thing is to enter the icon of the application, click, so that a black window appears, you must enter the writing or symbol of "greater than", or you can also press Alt+Ctrl+T.
- It provides the installation command mentioned above as "aircrack-ng", where you enter the command and press enter, the command is sudo apt-get install aircrack-ng.
- Enter the password when the software requires it, this is the key used to log in to the computer, then you can press "enter" and as such it enables root access, being useful to make the commands can be executed after the terminal.
- Locate the name on the monitor of the network you are looking to hack, at least a personal one should appear, otherwise it means that the WiFi card does not support this type of monitoring.
- Start monitoring the network by typing the command airmon-ng start and the network name and pressing enter.

- Enables the interface, after imposition of the iwconfig command.

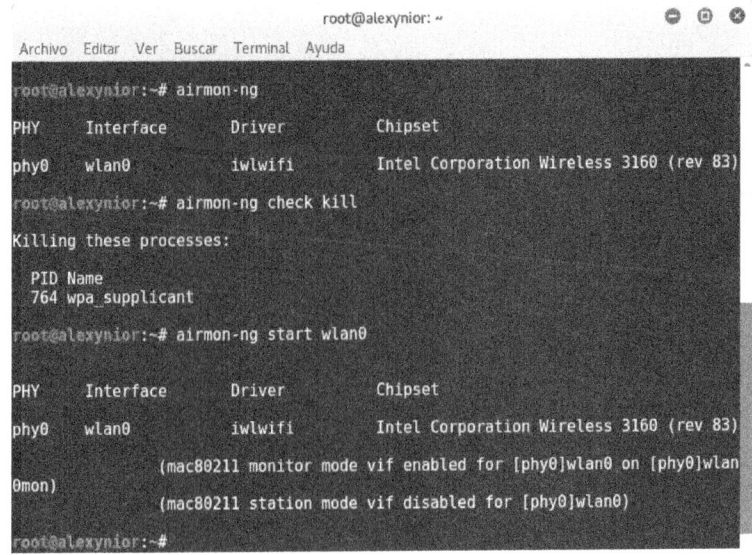

How to hack a WiFi network from Linux without a graphic card

The Linux method of hacking can be complex because of the graphics card issue, for that reason there are ways to perform this procedure when using aircrack-ng on a computer, but for this to become a reality, the following steps must be carried out:

1. **Downloading the dictionary file:** The most commonly used file for this purpose is Rock You, which can be downloaded, and then take into account the list of words, because if the WPA or WPA2 password is not on this result, it will not be possible to access the WiFi network.
2. **Start the password decryption procedure:** To start the progress, the command aircrack-ng -a2 -b MAC -w rockyou.txt name.cap must be included, it is essential to make sure to use the correct network information, in case it is a WPA network, change that "a2" for just an "a".
3. **Wait for the terminal results:** When a header such as "KEY FOUND" appears, you can get the password.

With an extra installation, and with less efficiency, the hacking of the WiFi network can be carried out, without the need to have the WiFi card, that kind of facility should be enhanced to achieve the expected results.

What you need to know to hack WiFi from Android

The availability of some WiFi networks, causes that there is some temptation to decrypt their keys, this is possible to do from an Android even, there are several applications for this purpose, can be used easily to have the password of the network, and enjoy that connection.

The only conditions to have the advantage of decrypting keys, is by means of certain devices that have special features, usually rooted devices, with available storage, battery and memory for optimal results.

By means of a few steps, you can try to hack the WiFi network, so simple your mobile can be transformed into a means of computer attack, you just have to implement the following actions:

1. First of all, any of the following tools must be downloaded via Google Play or the App Store, so that you can install them on your devices.
2. It is vital to open the application, so that it can be executed.

3. Usually the first thing most of these tools do is to analyze each WiFi network, in the middle of a list all the connectivity options are displayed.
4. In each WiFi network there is a color that indicates the degree of blocking, this is a signal of the available possibility of hacking, it is a starting point to carry out the attack.
5. When clicking on the network to be hacked, the next thing to do is to click on "Connect".

WPS Connect		↻ ⓘ
🔒 [WPA2]	5gNYSAL DC:53:7C:64:B9:A2	▼ -79
🔒 [WPA2]	PS4-370CF11D819D 80:05:94:6D:3D:51	▼ -80
🔒 [WPA2]	MiFibra-229B 44:FE:3B:40:22:9D	▼ -80
🔒 [WPA2]	Invitado-7F36 72:CC:22:9C:7F:39	▼ -83
🔒 [WPA2]	-- Hidden network -- 44:FE:3B:3F:A9:72	▼ -84
🔒 [WPA2]	MiFibra-A96F 46:FE:3B:3F:A9:72	▼ -84
🔒 [WPA2]	HUAWEI-E5186-5G-4F2B A4:CA:A0:4C:4F:2D	▼ -85
🔒 [WPA2]	ONOC825 DC:53:7C:3C:2D:3E	▼ -85
🔒 [WPA2]	forfox2 98:DE:D0:C3:5F:3F	▼ -85
🔒 [WPA2]	MiFibra-7F36 64:CC:22:9C:7F:38	▼ -85
🔒 [WPA2]	MiFibra-2F2F 44:FE:3B:40:2F:31	▼ -86
🔒 [WPA2]	Lowi4932 10:C2:5A:FB:49:37	▼ -86
🔒 [WPA2]	MiFibra-7274 BC:30:D9:79:72:76	▼ -89

You need to know the best Android apps for hacking WiFi networks, any of the following that you use, provides interesting results to breach network security levels:

- **Kali Linux NetHunter**

A tool of the stature of Kali Linux Nedthunter, is characterized by being one of the powerful, allows hacking any type of WiFi network, its operation is open source, is one of the pioneers in this area, to use it, you must have installed the Kali WiFi tool, to carry out the procedure.

Subsequently a custom Kernel must be incorporated, where the wireless injections are added, although some are not supported by certain Android, you should try to download the appropriate ones.

- **WPS Connect**

This is one of the most popular applications for hacking WiFi, its main theme is to test the security of the network, this application is compatible with routers of all kinds, the main thing is to install the application to use it in the detection of vulnerabilities available on a network.

The effectiveness of this application leans on the networks that are more vulnerable to hacking, which is carried out by means of PIN combinations, taking advantage of that probability that is generated by users who do not modify the password imposed by the router, that predetermined configuration is an advantage to connect to that network.

- **WPS WPA Tester**

This other alternative allows hacking the WiFi network, its development is based on making the most of the vulnerabilities it detects, in theory this function seeks to bring to light these flaws to fix them, but it is not controlled to be used for other purposes, for them you can try algorithms such as Belkin, TrendNet and the like.

The compatibility of the application, is associated with Android 5.0 version as well as higher versions, otherwise older versions do not help to detect the WEP-WPA-WPA2, and make fatal different attempts so that this can work.

- **Aircrack-ng**

A reliable and stable option to decrypt the WiFi network key is represented by this application, it is developed under the Linux kernel operation, its design is associated with XDA, for that reason it has an efficient use on Android, besides being able to find WiFi chips that are supported by the monitor mode.

The use of this application depends on a rooted device, also the assistance of a computer with Linux is key, to complete the proper use of each function, you can watch different tutorials that illustrate this use.

- **DSploit**

It has been developed as a great application for this purpose of studying WiFi networks, with an XDA quality, reaching the extreme of knowing the vulnerabilities that may exist on a WiFi network, being a great clue to penetrate the WiFi network, so it can be defined as a comprehensive package that analyzes and issues network information.

The capacity of this study allows to decipher more details of the WiFi, since a scan of the ports is carried out, without forgetting to track other kinds of operations, the use of this application is frequently explained by means of YouTube.

- **AndroDumpper**

AndroDumpper is presented as an application that scans WiFi networks that are nearby, it is a comprehensive description about the connection, it operates thanks to an algorithm that is set in motion to the point of determining some passwords, making possible the hacking that every user is looking for.

The operation of this application is directly associated with routers for WPS, although in other types of router can take effect, it is only a key requirement to use a rooted cell phone.

Android hacking can be complicated at first, but the above applications are the best for this mission, but at the beginning you should set up the application to be used from your own network or one to which you have access, then you can move on to another type of use.

Discover how to hack WPA and WPA2 networks without using a dictionary

The hacking of a WPA and WPA2 network is an ease, it is carried out by means of techniques that become automated, towards that kind of evolution is the WiFiPisher tool, it is a great novelty and it is part of the LINSET (Linset Is Not a Social Enginering Tool) design.

This kind of scripts follows the same process as other similar scripts, this is expressed after the following actions or attributions:

- Scan over nearby WiFi networks.

- It provides a list of available networks where filters can be incorporated.
- Network selection function to capture the handshake, in some cases can be used without handshake.
- Allows you to create the fake ap, in this step you can put the same name as the original, so that users can connect to this fake ap.
- DHCP server setup, this is incorporated on the fake network so that the victim's connection request gets a password request, when entered, the objective is achieved, this step can be customized to be the same as the victim's router.
- The password is verified and compared with the handshake, and if it is correct, the DoS attack is stopped and the server is downgraded to connect to the real AP again.

At the end of each of these functions, it is again time to clean up the temporaries that have been created, i.e. all services can be stopped so that there is no more execution by the system.

The use of LINSET to hack WPA and WPA2 networks, helps this process does not require dictionary, with the benefits of being in Spanish, and in the same file are included others, in the middle of this operation provides support to the community, without losing sight of the knowledge about the router manufacturer.

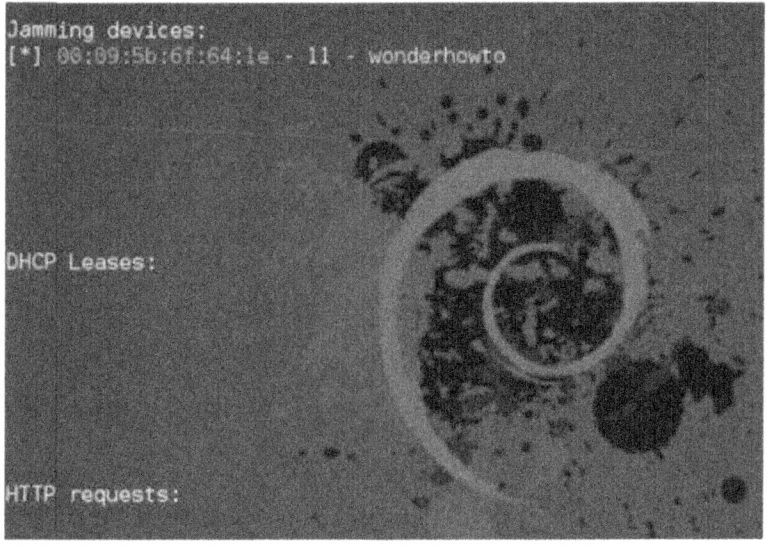

Each portal has languages accessible to each user, and develops different ways to capture the handshake, it is a tool with a much more mature design time, you must previously carry out these preparation actions:

1. Installation of each of the files mentioned above.
2. Customize the portal to be held captive, once you have the files separately.
3. Monitoring of the parameters to automate the attack to be performed.
4. There is no need to be obsessed with getting the handshake.

Hacking of WiFi networks with PMKID

WiFi network hacking techniques extend to different tools that focus on a different class of routers, such as PMKID password cracking, which has an optimal performance on WPA/WPA2 protocols, mastering every feature.

This kind of actions, seeks to alter WiFi networks, its functions were designed accidentally, trying to achieve the WPA3 security standard, that is why this method that allows to obtain and recover passwords arose, so it is attractive on hacking and especially for monitoring communications on the Internet.

The methods to reach a promising result, are presented when some user logs in, as he will be providing the password, all this happens after the 4-way authentication protocol, where the network port is checked, which translates into the following steps:

1. Use hcxdumptool tools, under v4.2.0 or higher, that way the PMKID generates the specific access point, to have contact with the received frame through a file.
2. Through the hcxpcaptool tool, the output is presented in pcapng format, where the hash format is converted and accepted by Hashcat.

3. Application of Hashcat password cracking tools, until the WPA PSK password is obtained, this type of password is extracted by the wireless network, but it only works or has more weight on networks with a roaming function.

This type of WiFi hack is not useful against a security protocol of the WP3 generation, because it is a more complicated modality to attack or breach, however, this technology is used against the one that already has more time of use or in the market.

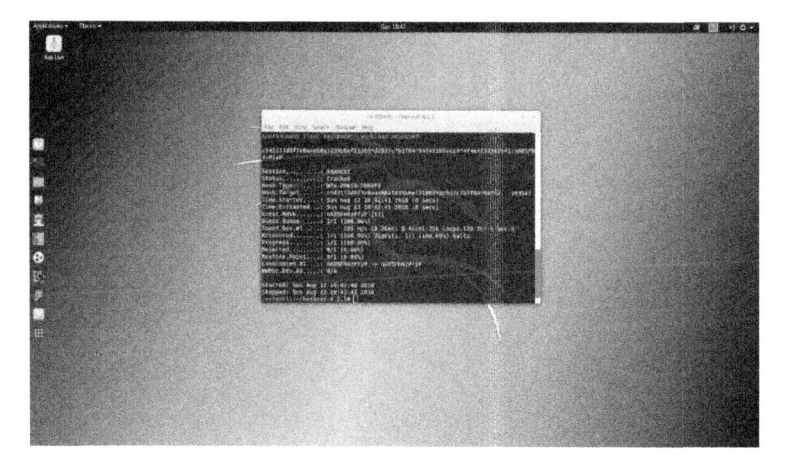

How to obtain WiFi network keys with BlackTrack 5

Blacktrack is known worldwide as a classic tool to carry out cracking, its operation is based on a distribution of the Linux system, its design is directly focused on carrying out these attacks, although at the official level it is published as a WiFi network auditing tool.

Over time, different versions of this program have been developed, along with a long list of tutorials, all of which can be found on its official website. It retains a wide variety of utilities within a single program, including the network scanner Nmap, Wireshark, and the browser exploit BeEF, which causes an extraction.

Its use is totally simple, and can be used on Windows as a boot system, then installed without problems, it is even available to be used on Android, but it is not recommended because it does not generate efficient results, where the first step is to be told by the type of network you want to attack.

```
bt ~ # airmon-ng
Interface       Chipset         Driver
ra0             Ralink b/g      rt2500
bt ~ # airmon-ng stop ra0

Interface       Chipset         Driver
ra0             Ralink b/g      rt2500 (monitor mode disabled)
bt ~ # ifconfig ra0 down
bt ~ # macchanger --mac 00:11:22:33:44:55 ra0
Current MAC: 00:c0:ca:25:2d:41 (Alfa, Inc.)
Faked MAC:   00:11:22:33:44:55 (Cimsys Inc)
bt ~ # airmon-ng start ra0

Interface       Chipset         Driver
ra0             Ralink b/g      rt2500 (monitor mode enabled)
bt ~ #
```

To evaluate the hacking options, you just need to check the panel of available WiFi networks, then copy the name of the network, and start the hacking procedure, the duration of the process carries out an estimation about the feasibility of hacking this type of network.

The secrets to hack WiFi networks without programs

There is no doubt that a simple step to hack a WiFi network, is not having to use programs, much less pay for such results, the first can be simply capturing some oversight on an open network without any configuration, it is not hacking properly, but it is simpler and lawful.

To capture some type of network without keys, it is necessary to acquire a long range WiFi antenna, its value is at least 100 euros, and then think about an installation on the terrace or rooftop, being able to detect any type of signal at least 5 km, and 20 km maximum, it is most useful if you have a central address.

The places with the greatest variety of public WiFi, can be dominated by means of this method, and the best of all is that it is a legal method, to carry it out you can know the following antennas on the market:

- **TP-Link TL-ANT2424B Antenna**

It meets a performance of 2.4GHz 300Mbps 9dB, is a solution so that no network can be overlooked outside, its application can be developed centrally, and emits a professional connection function, however its design is simple to understand, being a great alternative for companies as well as for homes.

- **Ubiquiti LBE-M5-23 - 5 GHZ**

LiteBeam M is based on a device known as airMAX, has lightweight features and an opportunity cost, in exchange for a high range connectivity, thanks to the application of a directional antenna that becomes immune to noise, as for the physical, consists of 3 axes that are easy to assemble.

This tool can be integrated without any problem to the pole, all thanks to its compact capacity that facilitates its application, it is a convenience to use this kind of powerful antenna.

- **Ubiquiti PowerBeam M 22dBi 5GHz 802.11n MIMO 2x2 TDMA**

It has a focus towards any direction of interest, helping to block any kind of interference, this immunity is useful in areas or spaces where different signals concur that hinder the capture of the networks, this design avoids confusion between the frequency, as it has Ubiquitis Innerfeed technology.

A positive aspect of this antenna is that it has no cable, since the feed is created by means of a radio in the horn, and at the same time this feature increases the performance, since there are no connection losses unlike cables.

Through these before you can get those WiFi networks that are open, in a matter of seconds and without much effort that connection arises, it is an investment that can open the doors towards that direction.

Acrylic, WEP and WPA WiFi network hacking

The Acrylic program plays the role of a wireless network analyzer, it works directly on Windows, has a variety of versions that achieve the purpose of finding passwords, everything is generated under an automated mode through the creation of scripts provided by the program.

Each script seeks to generate passwords, as they are programmed to do so, and are able to add information about new routers, everything is developed based on the security flaws it is able to discover, its use naturally corresponds to a protection on WiFi networks, but at the same time it is able to hack them.

This allows you to visualize the security options promoted by that WiFi network, thanks to the development of a driver to capture in monitor mode, the incidents of the WiFi network, each router model is analyzed by this tool, the first thing is that it detects the name of the network or SSID, as well as the MAC address, and type of security.

Any access point that is discovered by this tool, is due to the router's defects, being exploited by the program that is responsible for automatically calculating the passwords, and on this is concentrated the number of scripts that obtain a generic password, the accuracy increases after each version of the program.

With the results provided by this type of program, you can test passwords one by one, thus you can verify if they make possible the connection to the WiFi network, although its focus is to protect the network, in that same effectiveness is able to detect security flaws on other WiFi networks.

Among the commercial versions, Acrylic WiFi Professional is the most widely used, as a management of Acrylic WiFi Home, so that you can exercise the analysis on the WiFi network, and another alternative is the WiFi sniffer, which displays the traffic on a WiFi network, but also has security data to optimize the network.

Before any download, you can consult the official website of Acrylic WiFi, in addition to finding the professional version of this software, there are options for you to get more effective functions, it is best to open the program under the "continue trial" button to start the process.

Once you have clicked on this option, it is time to select the "create new" window, and then click on "open existing" to load the project, it is time to enter the data of the WiFi network, in addition to the map of the analyzed area, without forgetting to calibrate the map, and in the "plots" options, you have access to "access points" and "routes".

Rainbow tables as a password cracking technique

In recent years, the methods of hacking WiFi networks have become more complicated, based on the structure of the password, since when it is not a predetermined one, the function of the programs does not become effective, for this reason, new techniques can be implemented so that the password can be unveiled.

The solution to the problems of better structured passwords is to apply a mixed action, divided between dictionary and brute force, that is what Rainbow tables are composed of, so that the password combinations can arise by means of an algorithm, this operation helps to compare the password to be cracked.

This kind of technique relieves the pressure imposed on the computational load and increases the speed of cracking, which is a higher value than the others, thus improving the capabilities of the hardwares designed for this type of task.

Get to know the KRACK tool for hacking WiFi networks

The potential to find weaknesses on WPA2 networks, beyond its security level, the action of KRACK is very useful, for this you must discover the functions that this tool has, being a hacking method to take into account, its attack works on any WPA2 network.

The vulnerability that this program is able to find, has to do with the WiFi system itself that is being affected, directly as a condition of the manufacturer, also the hacking of a WiFi network can be implemented from the reinstallation of key by means of an Android device.

These paths help to decrypt each of the data transmitted by the user, this becomes very thorough on systems such as Linux, and also in Android 6.0 as well as later ones, as they face a phishing or ransomware, this process broadly covers 4 ways of the WPA2 security protocol.

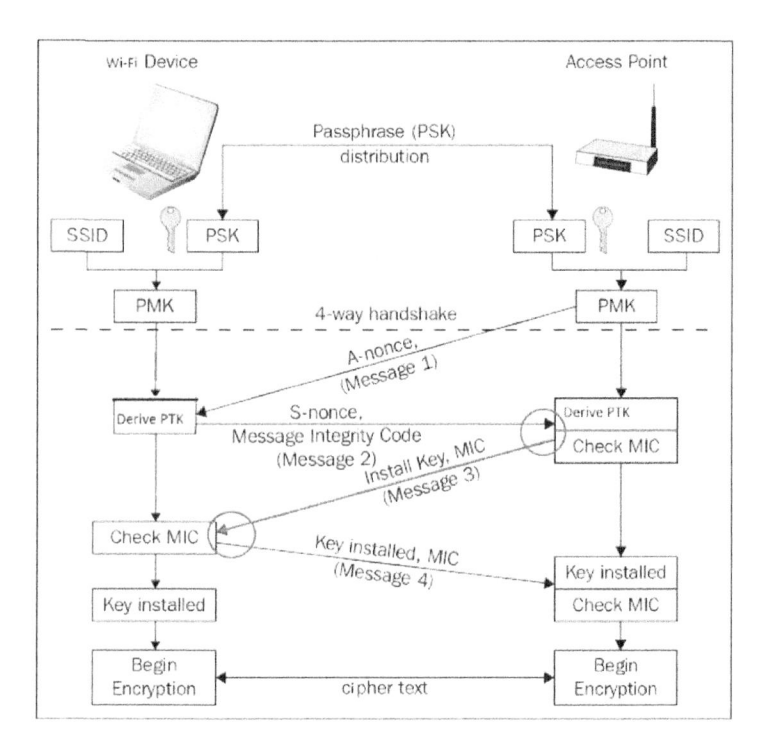

Diagram: 4-way handshake between Wi-Fi Device and Access Point, showing PSK distribution, PMK derivation, Message 1 (A-nonce), Message 2 (S-nonce, MIC), Message 3 (Install Key, MIC), Message 4 (Key installed, MIC), followed by encryption.

The program behind this acronym is defined as "Key reinstallation attack", being one of the most devastating forms of hacking, because beyond studying the traffic on a WiFi network, it is also responsible for forging and deploying packets, causing it to be effective on 41% of users.

WiFite WiFi network cracker

A tool like WiFit Wireless Auditor, has taken its time to improve its design since 2011, but has reached version 2 (r85), is an important contribution to test to impact any type of WiFi network, has a design for Linux, as well as being tested on BackBox, Pentoo, Blackbuntu, and also Backtrack 5.

A doubtful aspect is that it is not supported, however, it is tempting to measure its potential, because it provides a customized function that facilitates automation, it does not need many arguments or explanations, it immediately becomes a standard program to perform wireless auditing.

However, you must take into account the requirements of this program, which include the following:

1. Python 2.6.X or Python 2.7.X.
2. Patched wireless driver to generate monitor mode, along with injection, because security distributions have pre-patched wireless drivers.
3. Have installed the aircrack-ng 1.1 suite.
4. Keep Reaver installed for support, causing the attack on WPA2 networks to take place, this is made possible by WPS.

Once each of these requirements are met, the next step is to download and install the application, for which permissions must be granted to facilitate its execution, this is expressed by means of the command "chmod +x wifite.py", until the application is executed, in case of any doubt, it is best to access the "help" option.

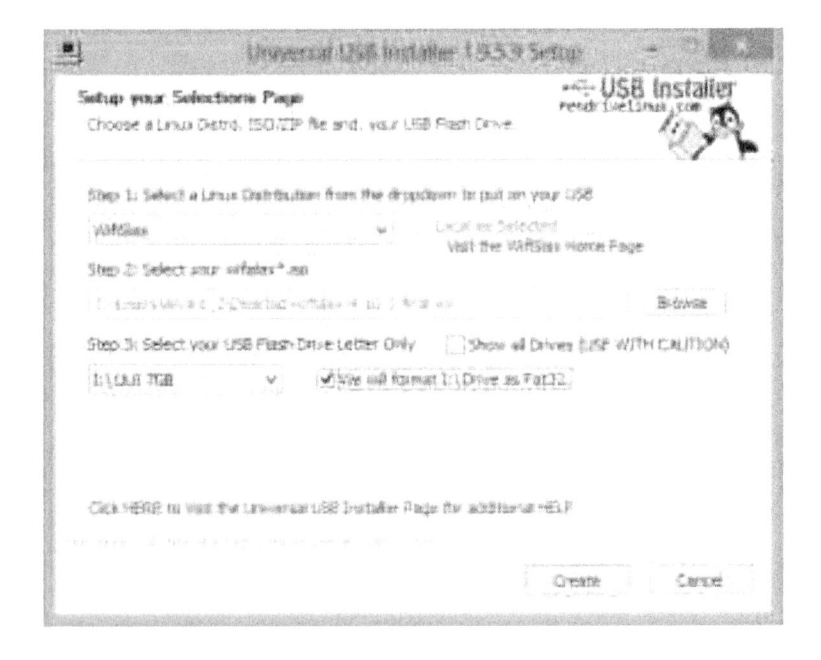

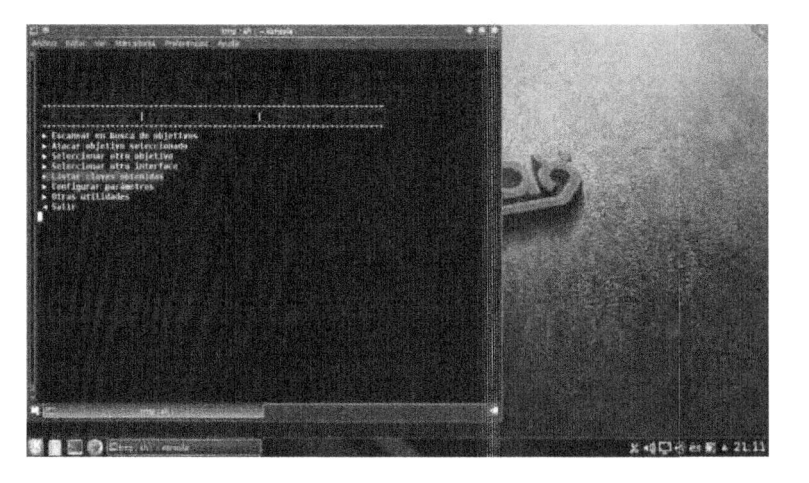

The essential thing is that you can have affinity for the application of filters, and other functions at the time of scanning, but in general terms its development is simple, once started, is responsible for scanning each of the networks automatically, provides information on the available channels, is a waiting phase until it ends.

During the scanning process, you must press CRTL+C, then the program itself requires the network number you are interested in auditing, and then the functions take care of providing the WiFi network key, which is why it is classified as a program that meets anyone's expectations.

On WPA2 networks that have WPS enabled, this program works great, but for the security level it has a slow development, however it is associated with the Reaver file, as more versions are presented, you get a solution for any hacking plan.

Hacking WiFi networks using Wifimosys

The tools to hack WiFi networks are becoming easier to use, one of them is Wifimosys, it has been considered as a kind of Linset 2.0, it is ideal for those who do not have much knowledge in computer science, it is a great start to attack WiFi networks, since it has an ideal interface.

The purpose of this tool is the same as Linset, in fact it is derived from the installation of Wifislax, and for this you must perform the following steps:

- Open Wifimosys, via Start/Wifislax/WPA/Wifimosys.

```
#########################################################
#                                                       #
#            WIFIMOSYS 0.22 by Absolut Vodker            #
#                   WIFI MOron' SYStem                   #
#                                                       #
#  Basado en LINSET de vk496 para seguridadwireless.net  #
#                                                       #
#########################################################

Elige escaneo de canal(es):

1) Todos los canales
2) Canal(es) específico(s)
3) Salir

#>
```

- Start the tool that puts the WiFi antenna in monitor mode.
- Execution of the scan to find the channels that are available.
- Once the WiFi networks can be found, the next thing to do is to press CRTL+C.

```
                    LISTADO DE REDES

 N°   MAC              CANAL   TIPO    PWR    NOMBRE DE LA RED

 1*   ...                1     WPA2    63%    ...
 2    ...                7     WPA2    73%    ...
 3    ...                7     WPA2    0%     Nombre oculto
 4    ...               13     WPA2    106%   MISO
 5    ...                9     WPA2    98%    ...
 6*   ...                9     WPA2    70%    ...
 7*   ...                9     WPA2    70%    ...
 8    ...                9     WPA2    0%     ...
 9    ...                9     WPA2    60%    ...

 (*) En rojo: redes con posibles clientes activos

 Selecciona el nº de la red a atacar...
 (Para reescanear pulsa r Para salir pulsa x)

 #> 4
```

Once the network is identified, it is time for the capture function to be performed, just press enter so that the process goes automatically, exercising an attack where the password can be retained, thus completing this simple action, although it is a lengthy process.

Jumpstart for hacking WiFi networks from Windows

The operation of applications or programs to hack WiFi networks from Windows, is a requirement given the large number of users who have this operating system, the solution is to think of Jumpstart along with Dumpper, although its operation is not entirely accurate, it is a great help to try to break the WiFi network.

To have access to the use of this tool, the first thing to do is to download it, but first you must unzip the Dumpper, so that access can be guaranteed, although its operation only materializes when there is a vulnerability on the WPS, but you can try to start the Dumpper tool.

Therefore the program itself broadcasts the nearby networks, and allows to press the option to expose the pin of those networks, only the ones that appear must be saved, at this point, the help of an external antenna is notorious, so that the JumStart can be executed, to start the third option of enter the pin fron my Access point.

It is necessary to paste a pin of the selected connection, it is essential to perform this step under a strict order, then in the lower zone is the option Automatically select network, this is destilda and press next, to continue with the selection of the connection, to see if the process has been successful, saving the data obtained.

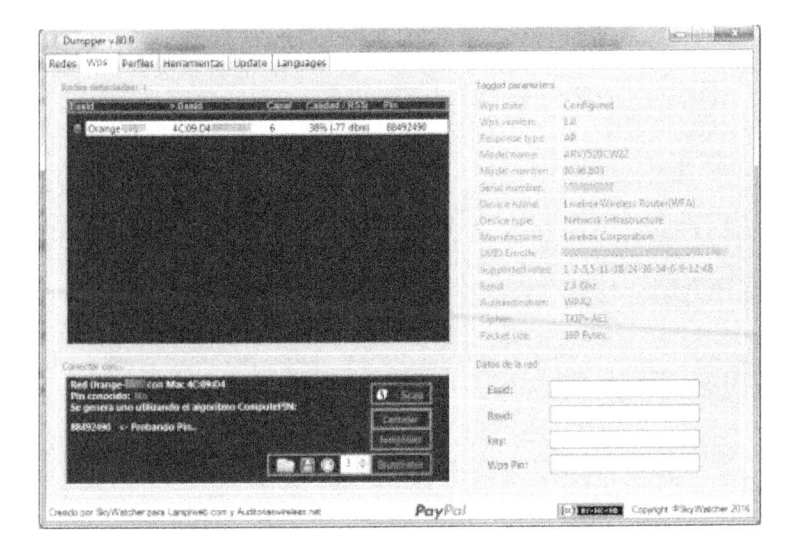

Sometimes it is necessary to carry out several attempts, in addition to alternating with different networks, it is better to use each of the pins, in case it does not work the first time, the essential thing is to try until it connects.

Decrypting the WiFi key on a Mac

A method compatible with a Mac system, is the KISMAC program, this helps to carry out the hacking of the WiFi network, it is based on a function that has a long history, for this you must install the program and then run its functions, then when it is installed, you must go to the preferences option, and then click on Driver.

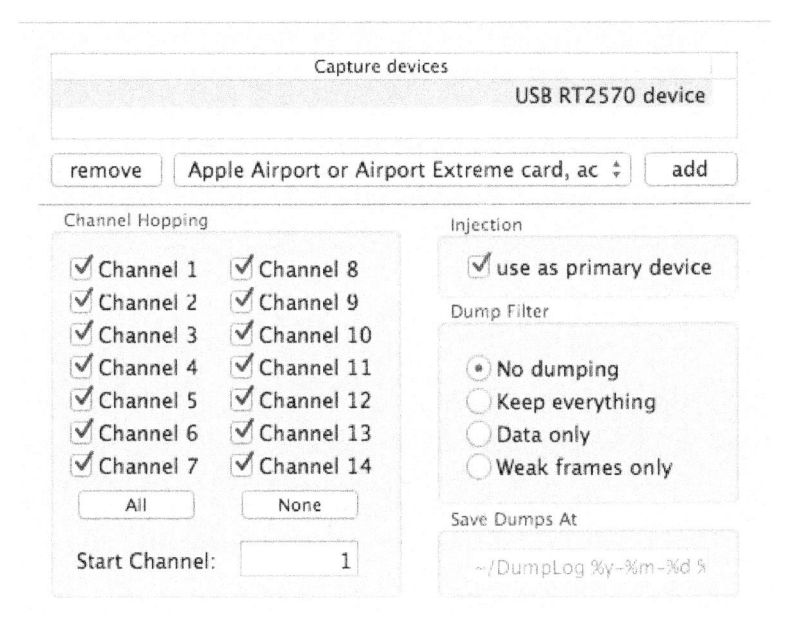

Then you must select the capturer, this is responsible for taking advantage of some gap, and in "add", the action of an external WiFi antenna is included, before the channel selection, it is best to choose all, and then close the preferences window, the next thing is to perform start scan, where the super administrator provides the key to connect.

This type of process is much more time-consuming, so it is better to let other activities to be managed, since it is necessary to complete an exchange of 150,000 packets, being part of the unveiling of the HandShake, and finding it exposes the networks that could not be found.

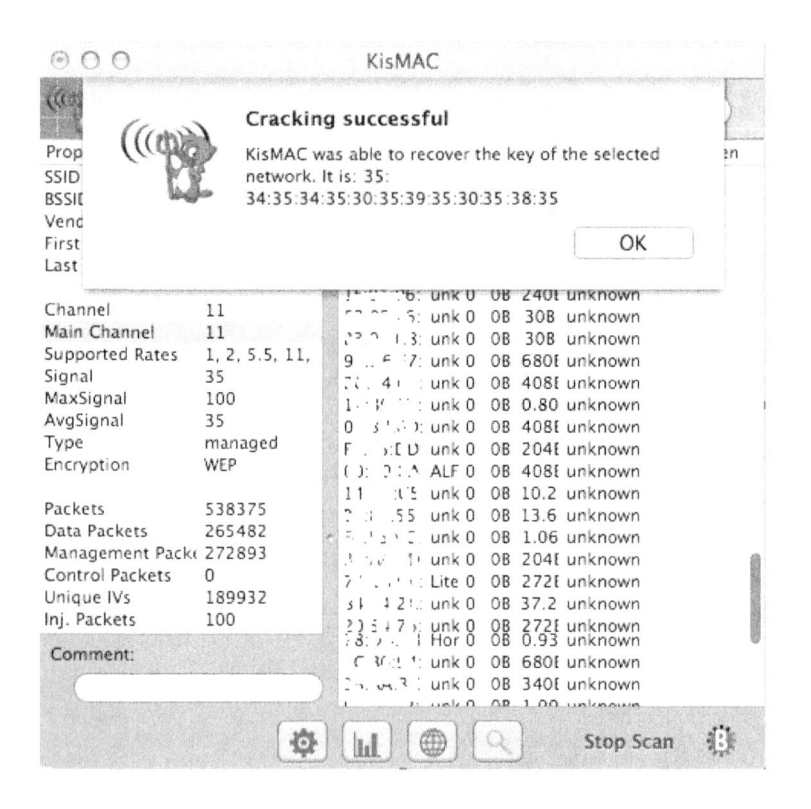

Once the Handshake is discovered, the WPA dictionary is loaded, when it is located the program itself is responsible for carrying out the attack, this tool is simple and effective to use as a way of hacking WiFi networks, it is an opportunity for a Mac to carry out this process.

Advanced tools for auditing WiFi networks

Currently there are different tools to perform an inspection on WiFi networks, such systems are used to unveil keys, as has been reiterated, these functions are available to anyone with just a pre-installation, as well as access from different systems.

One of the most widely used tools to break WiFi networks, is the WiFi network scanner, it is an application that is available for both Android and iOS, likewise the use on computers can be more comfortable for most, the simplicity of this installation opens all the doors to think about this alternative.

Every access point in the vicinity will be detected, which means that you can have data, signal level or strength, encryption and the MAC address of the AP, that kind of advantage over weak security protocols, such as WEP, and the same goes for WPA.

In the case of using operating systems such as Windows, the best choice as a scanner is Acrylic WiFi, is a professional mode to carry out the creation of scripts, this one of the various tools that extend to a mobile use, it all depends on the way that is more practical.

The information provided by the scanner is what helps to hack some network, in the case of wanting to perform these steps from Android devices, the answer lies on WiFi Analyzer, being a great solution because it has a free mode, being useful for 2.4 GHz and even 5 GHz band access.

For a use through iOS devices, you can download Network Analyzer Pro, although it is not a free option, but that means it provides advanced features, it marks a big distinction unlike some Android app.

Among the most important tools for penetrating WiFi networks are the following:

- **WirelessKeyView:** It represents a tool that has a positive level of utility, is free and is responsible for recreating a list of WEP, WPA2, and WPA keys, using each piece of data that is stored by the computer.
- **Aircrack-ng:** This is a suite of open source applications, each one is designed to hack WEP

and WPA/WPA2 keys, it is compatible with any type of system and its functions are extensive.

Beyond these tools, Wi-Fi Sniffers are a much more efficient method of retaining information about APs, retaining the packets that are shared over the network, and this traffic data can be imported into the aforementioned tools.

Decrypt WiFi passwords stored on the cell phone

Entering certain WiFi network passwords on the mobile, can bring inconveniences in the future such as forgetting them, or wanting to return to that place and have the password to enter it on another kind of device, in this scenario, it is possible to decrypt the key, both Android and Apple devices.

Each device stores an infinite amount of data, in the middle of the information are the WiFi network accesses, since that kind of storage is what allows them to connect automatically, thus increasing the chances of retrieving that kind of data by developing a specific process for that mission.

- **For non-rooted Android mobile devices**

One of the advantages of modern Android systems such as; Android 10 or Android 11, it is much easier to view the keys, without any need for root, to make this happen, you just have to share the network through the QR code, thus the information is compressed through this way, where is also the password.

Through this way, the system itself generates a QR code, allowing from another device can be scanned, for this you can use applications designed for this function, on different devices do not need to download anything because the system itself includes it, being part of brands such as Xiaomi, Samsung and others.

The creation of the QR code is carried out by means of a simple process as follows:

1. Enter the cell phone settings.
2. Navigate to the WiFi connections, and find the network you want to recover or know its password again.
3. In the options that are displayed on that network, you must look for the QR code symbol, when you click on it, an image with the code is created.
4. The transmitted or generated image must be captured to save the QR code, in the middle of this information is

included the name of the WiFi network, known as SSID, in addition to the password, which is precisely what you are looking for.

5. In case you do not have a mobile device that does not allow you to generate QR code, you can capture the QR code using Google Lens, this tool opens when you press the Google Assistant, and in a square with a dot, the QR code capture is incorporated in the gallery.

This completes a very simple method, compared to what is involved in rooting a cell phone, because each condition of the cell phone makes the conditions or processes to find the password grow.

- **Decrypting WiFi keys through rooted cell phones**

Every Android phone stores each of the WiFi network keys by default, so you can access this data easily, there is no need to write down data in case it is lost, so it is essential to get this kind of information through the rooted device.

Having a rooted mobile, implies that you can have access to each record, this includes the issue of passwords, this is not easy, because it compromises the security of the mobile device, but it is a comprehensive management of the mobile, that allows you to use different apps that are compatible with that condition, such as the following:

1. **WiFi Key Recovery**

This application implements a method as simple as the previous one, you have access to the saved networks, to find those options where you have ever connected, so you only need to select the network that is of interest, so you can click on the option to share the key, creating the QR code or sending it to a friend.

- **Discovering WiFi network keys with root and file explorer**

With a device that has root access, there is also the possibility of recovering the WiFi password through the file explorer, this can usually be a Root Browser reading, for this permissions must be granted to the root to be able to explore each of the files.

The search of the files where the keys are, must be carried out by means of the command data/misc/wifi, until finding the file wpa.supplicant.conf. it must be opened through a text editor, then it must be executed to observe the WiFi networks together with the passwords, locating all that connection history of the past.

- **Key search via iOS**

Observing the passwords found in iOS systems is possible, although discovering these WiFi networks can be more complicated compared to Android, for this you need to have a macOS, in addition to having the iPhone synchronized directly in iCloud.

First of all, it is essential to have iCloud activated, for this you must go to settings, then to Apple ID, until you find the iCloud

Keychain, so you can check that everything is activated, although this sequence of steps depends on the type of iOS version with which the process is carried out.

Once iCloud is activated, it is time to go back to the settings, in that sector you can take into account the "internet sharing" option, now the process is directed to the Mac, to carry out the recovery action through these steps:

1. Connect the Mac computer to the access point, this is done via the iPhone and the WiFi menu options.
2. As the sync is generated, each of the passwords stored on the iPhone, start to link to the Mac computer.
3. Once you are on the Mac computer, it is time to open the keychain app.
4. You must go to the "system" option, which is located in the upper left part of the window.
5. It is time to click on the "passwords" option, which is located on the left side of the screen.
6. Selecting the above option brings up each of the networks that have connected to the iPhone, then you can choose the network you wish to discover or probe.
7. Next, click on the "show password" option.

8. Immediately the program prompts for the username and password, this allows you to act as an administrator, until the password you are looking for is issued.

Alternatives to hack WiFi networks

The control or vulnerability of WiFi networks, is developed under a wide variety of programs designed for that purpose, one of the most popular with a large number of downloads at present are the following:

- **WiFi WPS WPA Tester**

It is a very implemented and simple hacking tool for Android, its original idea is the recovery of lost keys of WiFi networks, its use is based on implementing a dictionary to find out the type of key compatible with that network, it is not an algorithm directly attack for legal issues.

The operation relies on the default information of the router manufacturers, that configuration is exploited to the maximum, testing or using the 13 attempts to find the password of the WiFi network, with the application of the information or data of these popular models.

- **Cain & Abel**

This way is indispensable when it comes to hacking, it is known in short as Cain, it has a great power to be used on Windows, it specializes in loading packets to perform a deep search, causing it to also be able to crack, using different password hashes.

Sniffing techniques are used, without leaving aside the action of cryptanalysis, it is an accompaniment of brute force as well as dictionary attacks, the tool breaks a capacity to capture and obtain passwords of WiFi networks, by studying the protocols that are in transfer.

It is unimaginable the amount of data that can be retained when this tool works, subsequently when using Cain, anyone finds weak points about the security of the WiFi network, each aspect is exposed by the tool, in principle with an informative orientation, and can be used as a hint to hack.

- **Kismet**

It is a packet capture tool, it is based on a hacking mechanism, it manifests the ability to analyze all kinds of aspect on the network, its main implementation is noted on the intruders that roam that type of connection, each function goes hand in hand with the WiFi card.

The rfmon mode supports monitoring over any network, no matter if they are hidden, as it highlights the wireless network protocols: 802.11a, 802.11b, 802.11g and even 802.11n, its availability is on operating systems such as Linux, Windows and BSD, so it can be run.

- **Airsnort**

The action on encrypted WiFi networks, is a reality through this tool, its intervention is passive, it is launched on WiFi connections, to seize the packets to get the encryption key of the network in just a few seconds, these features are similar to those of Aircrack.

The difference of this tool with the rest, is based on its interface, because its management is more open for any user, so there is no problem to take more control over the program, its download is free and available for Windows and Linux.

- **NetStumbler**

It represents an ideal alternative for Windows, the purpose is that this application can detect an access point, it is also designed to perform much more advanced functions on networks that are misconfigured, in the middle of a network there are a variety of options.

The version of this tool is free, and even has a minimalist mode as MiniStumbler, this is incorporated as a utility for any type of Windows user.

- **Airjack**

If you want to go beyond the hacking action, this tool is a great answer to take that step, its function is the injection of packets on any type of network, thus extracting the data, seeking that these vulnerabilities can be exploited to the maximum, generating access to network resources.

The management of this type of tool is outstanding, although initially it is to measure the security of a WiFi network, responding to the injection of false packets, it is a necessary download for this type of purpose.

- **inSSIDer**

Every detail about a WiFi network can be exposed thanks to this tool, not only hacking functions, but also a complete scanner to act on the wireless network in the appropriate or desired way, its design fulfills a variety of tasks, such as accentuating the access points of each WiFi network.

On the other hand, the signal is monitored, so that each record is collected to keep track of the wireless card data, which is one of the most important functions of this system.

- **CowPatty**

It is an option available for Linux systems, it is available to carry out audits about the security of the WiFi network, this is one of the most used for this purpose, its execution or action is based on a series of commands, where the use of dictionaries is executed in addition to brute force to breach all kinds of security.

When it comes to WiFi network security systems, the most usual thing is that it has positive results on WEP and WPA systems, so you can download this tool to take advantage of these aspects.

- **Wepttack**

The use of these tools does not stop for Linux, in fact it is where they are most effective, that is the case of this application, it is used to have an exclusive domain on this ecosystem, although its action is only specialized on WEP encryption, using this type of attacks by means of dictionary.

The central utility of this program is to keep track of security, causing the password can be obtained on the study of these networks, its purpose is to be a great answer to some forgetfulness of this type, is a thorough program in every way, but useful even for hacking purposes.

How to decrypt WiFi network passwords according to companies

One of the key or easy aspects that can be exploited to hack WiFi networks is the company, i.e. the internet operator is known as a vulnerability variable that can be studied in depth to perform the attack, also depending on the type of company the process changes, so knowing one by one is useful.

- **Decode Jazztel WiFi keys**

The figure of a Jazztel router, is a technological utility that requires maximum care, since it has a wide level of vulnerability, if the default built-in password does not change, it only means that many attacks will be originated, because anyone can be able to attack that security.

To check and take advantage of any opportunity, just download Router Keygen, then all you have to do is start its functions, then the process takes more than 2 seconds, even if you have changed the network password, you can use auditing systems such as WifiSlax or Wifiway.

This type of connection does not provide any kind of guarantee, the decryption of the key is carried out quickly, in addition to the fact that most of these networks do not have WPA2 encryption, i.e. the auditing systems work effectively when a password is not established.

In order to carry out any kind of attack, it is recommended that each user seeks to establish a complex password, since when combinations of uppercase, lowercase and symbols are imposed, it is very difficult to decipher the passwords.

- **Discover ONO company passwords**

ONO networks can be a target for hacking, it is better to opt for systems such as Wifislax, as it has a large margin of success, this helps any kind of vulnerability to be exploited to the maximum, although through Android there is also the possibility of carrying out a hack.

With the ONO4XX FREE Android application, you can attack a WiFi network, you only need a download to perform this step, although it is not as powerful as Wifislax, because the

Android mode only decrypts ONO router keys that are old, or those that have WEP or WAP keys, up to the default ones.

To recognize that it is the ONO company, you must identify the SSID, which normally has a nomenclature like the following:

1. ONOXXXXXXXX
2. ONOXXXX
3. ONOXAXA

This kind of study is useful, where the ONO4XX FREE app is responsible for exploiting the ONO router keys, which have the SSID ONOXXXXXX, ie not possessing letters but this description, because it means that they have an old security, which also has a resounding effect the type of MAC, as it is required to start with:

1. E0:91:53
2. 00:01:38

But when the network is not compatible with these details, you can still try to breach the security of the WiFi network, because the ONO router has great weakness to the action of Wifislax, because the algorithm that has the ONO password, has been leaked on most hacking designs.

ONO is considered as one of the secure operators, but leaves certain security criteria in the hands of attack intentions, although this company is currently above Vodafone, its Netgear routers provide acceptable performance, but without the basic configuration, they are still easy networks to attack.

- **Decrypt Movistar WiFi network passwords**

Movistar WiFi routers are classified as one of the easiest to hack, and its SSID is very accessible to verify, and in most cities is a common service, to this is added a long list of Android apps that allow the decoding of the keys of such networks.

Movistar as one of the operators to take into account, the hacking opportunity is based on the serial configuration of their routers, because when the WPS is enabled it complicates everything, so the use of the Androdumpper application, as well as the Wifislax program has an optimal result to retain the desired password.

It is very quick to discover the WiFi network key, because the longer it takes to disable the WPS, the better the chance of gaining access to the WiFi network, especially if high-density keys are not set up.

- **Decrypt Vodafone WiFi network passwords**

In a time span from 2014 to 2015, Vodafone WiFi networks were no impediment to any hacking purpose, as the information was fully leaked, causing the algorithm it uses to be known by the entire online community, so any user who owns a router prior to 2015, is a resounding risk.

In any location where there is a predetermined key, it is easy to hack WiFi networks, the vulnerability is a factor that cannot be overlooked, since programs such as Router Keygen has the algorithm of this company, although with routers that are new, the hacking process becomes complicated.

The best way to decrypt a WiFi network of this company, is through the Kali Linux tool, along with its application "WifiPhisher", being an advanced hacking method, through these methods a variety of attacks are managed, the action of WifiPhisher is based on creating a fake access point.

As the action of the Vodafone router can be blocked, so that the user can issue his password, the lime is decrypted for a malicious purpose, that kind of obtaining is part of the power of WifiPhisher that acquires the new password, for them pop-ups are a lure to reach that password.

Such a method works with a striking level of effectiveness over another type of network, as Vodafone is not the only company at risk of being hacked by the leaked data.

• **Get WiFi network keys with Orange**

For those looking to decode an Orange WiFi key, there are a lot of opportunities to carry out this procedure, one of the most prominent is through the Android application PulWifi, it is based on a simple mechanism that allows to observe in green the networks that are vulnerable.

In the middle of the analysis of this application, in red color are those that are not possible to hack, this is due to the fact that this application has the design loaded with the algorithm of Orange WiFi networks, so it dominates most of the keys that have the Orange WiFi routers by default.

On the other hand, in order to breach WiFi networks, you can run the WirelessCracker tool, since it has a similar operation to Pulwifi, you only need to take advantage of SSID recognition, to exploit the weakness of each company, in the case of Orange there is that vulnerable percentage.

Preferably, the use of Pulwifi has better results, because it provides notifications when there is a possibility of a breach, since it focuses on a WiFi network that it can decode effectively, by means of the Orange WiFi passwords information it has stored.

- **Decode Claro's WiFi networks**

In the middle of WiFi networks that are part of Claro, the most effective way out is to use Turbo WiFi, especially as a useful tool for the large number of countries where Claro operates, given the large number of Claro areas, this is a key solution, on the other hand, you can incorporate the operation of Wifi Unlocker as a great tool for this.

In the midst of hacking attempts, the action of an APK can be added, the better strategies are incorporated, the better results are presented, because the WiFi network itself receives attacks from different fronts.

The best way to hack WiFi networks, step by step

In the different methods that exist to hack WiFi networks, each one has its ease or complication, it all depends on the basic knowledge of the user, but the important thing is to recognize that each way, is a failure or neglect of the security of the connection itself.

The initial steps to hack a WiFi network at a general level, and based on the Wifislax program, are as follows:

1. First of all, you must have the Wifislax system download, its function is to audit computer networks, and it is very useful to obtain data of this nature.

2. Once you have downloaded Wifslax, it is time to transfer it to a USB memory stick, using a special program that allows you to convert this storage into a bootable system.
3. Connect the USB flash drive to the computer, then turn on the computer, to start the Wifislax boot, without causing any damage.
4. Once you start Wifislax, there is an opportunity to hack into the WiFi network using these audit-based tools.

In order for this procedure to be carried out efficiently, it is important to have a computer, although these steps are not suitable for an Apple Mac, but the repeated requirement that is imposed as a requirement is the WiFi card, looking for it to be compatible with the audit functions.

The recommendation to have this requirement covered, is to have the Alfa Network USB WiFi adapter, it is based on an adapter that works through a chip, helping the hacking tools to be fully utilized, the first thing is to test the chip on the computer.

On the other hand, the role of the USB flash drive is important, since that 8 GB capacity as a recommendation, is the one that will contain the system, causing each of the audit tools that are key to hacking to be installed, for best results you can implement a large capacity WiFi antenna.

These initial steps are the ones that allow to carry out any hacking plan, and the availability of Wifislax can be 32 or 64 bits, to convert the pendrive into a bootable system, it is best to use the UnetBootIn program, where the ISO is added, but once the program is installed, the only thing left to do is to use its tools.

Starting the program allows you to find all the available options, where the same Windows startup appears but with a Linux theme, just click on "run command", then it is time to enter the command "geminis auditor", this is a tool that helps to scan every available WiFi network within reach.

The networks that are emitted in green, are accessible to hack, to attack it, click on the option to attack target, the same tool provides two options, you can run both to generate the issuance of the password of the WiFi network, the path for this is "opt/GeminisAuditor".

This command is responsible for creating a file with all the passwords that have been decrypted, to make use of them, you must open a file from the browser, another type of tool that provides the program is Linset being another of the functions of this comprehensive program, which can be fully explored.

Kali Linux: the most effective hacking of networks

When mentioning methods to hack WiFi networks, it is impossible to leave aside an operating system designed for this function, that is why it is one of the most popular options, it also has different ways of installation, it can be on the computer and in the middle of the boot disk.

This kind of response or measure, which can be executed on a computer, known as VMWare, Virtual Box and other options, stores an important variety of computer forensic tools, among which Kismet and Aircrack-ng stand out, allowing pentesting in WiFi networks.

This type of system has a free mode, its web support is really positive to take into account, and online circulates an important variety of content to start working with this tool from scratch, it stands out for including the following tools:

- **Reaver:** It is an action that allows hacking any network through the WPS, especially when using PIN enabled, being effective on those networks that keep the WPS active.
- **Wi-FI Honey:** It is a tool that has the shape of a honeycomb, causing the effect of attracting users, as they want to connect to that access point, they acquire that data through the implementation of false APs, it is a capture of that type of traffic.
- **FreeRadius-WPE: It is** responsible for performing man-in-the-middle attacks, being ideal for 802.1 authentication as one of the targets.

Learn how to decrypt WiFi networks with Aircrack-ng

The use of aircrack-ng must be explained because it is one of the best tools, it has a great function or performance to hack WiFi networks, although for this you must have a wireless card, without leaving aside to have the Kali Linux distribution, to comply with these aspects, is to be ready to carry out the following actions:

1. **Adaptor preparation**

It is a phase of verification about Kali, is the identification of the adapter, this is possible through the terminal, where you run the command: airmon-ng, then it is time to disable any intervening process, for this you must place this command: airmong-ng check kill.

Subsequently, monitoring is activated by means of the command: airmon-ng start wlan0, for which the interface name must be identified, so that the airodump-ng can be started, thus each connection is studied.

2. **Find a target WiFi network**

When you have the list of nearby access points, you can implement the function of decrypting the password of the selected one, for this it is important to write down the BSSID and CH, then it is time to press the Crtl+C keys, thus executing the command airodump-ng -c 6 -bssid 02: 08: 22: 7E: B7: 6F - write (network name).

3. **Issue a deauth attack**

It is time to open a terminal, to generate the deauth attack, so that each user will be disconnected from that network, this creates an ideal scenario to obtain the handshake, once it is obtained, press Crtl+C again.

4. **Decrypt WiFi passwords by brute force**

This stage is dedicated to the unveiling of the key with the help of aircrack-ng, this should cause the KeyFound result to be returned, it all depends on the complexity of the key.

The fastest method to hack WiFi networks

The hacking of WiFi networks can be executed in a simple way, so the main trick tool to keep in mind is the WiFi Hack 2021 All In One program, it has been considered as the most effective way to breach the security of this connection, being a program compatible with Windows, MAC and Linux.

This type of utility can be used through Android and iPhone, through a download that is not entirely free, this is because it is not a simple process, and has real results, so it is a quick solution, effective but not economical for some users looking for a free way.

NetSpot for hacking vulnerable WiFi networks

The analysis to hack a WiFi network can be carried out with NetSpot, since its specialty is based on concentrating on that type of network that has a lower level of security, i.e. all the focus is on those that are protected and classified as WEP, being a big difference in resistance based on WPA or WPA2.

Finding networks that are protected by WEP means that you have in your hands an easy alternative for hacking, because you only need to install the appropriate software, let it act, and in a short time the WiFi network will be decrypted, NetSpot's action is important because it applies a discovery as a method of analysis.

In the middle of the reports provided by this tool, it presents all the details related to the adjacent WiFi networks, it is a great facility to see each of the names and identifications of the networks surrounding your devices, up to determine the signal level, the channels that emit data and security as well.

When a network with WEP security is highlighted, it is time to demonstrate the knowledge of hacking this type of network, the search for this type of network has been facilitated by this tool, which works at the same time to help protect a network, evaluating the security requirements.

How to crack the router's default password

The importance of the router is based on the fact that it is the source of connections itself, these are exposed to different types of malware that seek to take advantage of weak passwords, this is due in part to users who do not enter the router, i.e. its website, to change the password they provide by default.

The security of a connection depends on this step, the first thing to take into account is the IP address, as this is different for each router, and is what allows you to enter the administration interface of the same, that IP address is on the same router placed on a label.

But, this type of IP address can be found through sites like routeripaddress.com, being a source of information about a router's IP address, so with a few clicks, you have access to this type of information, the best example comes after the Linksys router, which has a common address of 192.168.1.1.

In the case of the Belkin router, its address is known as 192.168.2.2.2, so you can access its administration options:

-10.0.0.1

-10.0.1.1

- 192.168.2.1

- 192.168.11.1

- 192.168.0.1

- 192.168.0.227

By identifying the router manufacturer, it is possible to get to the bottom of the configurations, which is beneficial for exploiting these types of vulnerabilities, as well as certain tools mentioned above, which allow the discovery of this data, which is important for taking advantage of carelessness.

The default password to access the router configuration is usually "admin", but you can also use Google to find the login name and the default password for the model and manufacturer of the router, so that you can get more information to break the configuration.

Faults available behind the routers

No type of router is immune to vulnerabilities, because at the hardware and software level, especially when they do not have an active update system, they are still vulnerable and put the entire WiFi network at risk. More than 127 home routers have security flaws, causing unfortunate results.

To determine the vulnerability of a router, it is necessary to take into account certain details, the first is the date of its launch, to detect the type of firmware that has that model, to this is added the time that has the version of the operating system used, on the other hand, are the techniques that the router has to mitigate deception.

In the market, by statistics and study, it has been determined that 46 of them have not had updates in recent years, causing a great weakness to attacks of all kinds, without leaving aside the models that issue updates without patching known vulnerabilities, so it is a great margin of hackeble option.

The best brands that meet these criteria are ASUS and Netgear, while D-Link, TP-Link, Zyxel and Linksys, this is because the first two brands have 13 accessible private keys, which means that no attacker can have them, while if the key is in the firmware, the key is present on these models.

More than 90% of routers use the Linux system, and this type of system is not constantly updated, only 5% of them have an update support until 2022, but when it comes to avoid buying a router, Linksys WRT54GL stands out, as it is one of the most vulnerable in the market.

The weakness of the aforementioned model is due to the fact that its design corresponds to 2002, and some users keep it or even acquire it because of its low cost, so using an old router is a significant danger, thus, by knowing the brand of the router, it is possible to determine in advance the difficulty to hack.

Tips and requirements for hacking WiFi networks

Dedicating yourself to the hacking of a WiFi network is undoubtedly a time-consuming action, but so that it is not a wasted effort, you can follow the following recommendations to carry out an effective process:

- **Check the capacity of your equipment**

It is vital to take into account the type of mechanisms you have to use a hacking tool, since having a WiFi card is a key requirement for a process with better results, in case you do not have it, what you can do is to have a card connected via USB.

On the other hand, in addition to the WiFi card, the WiFi antenna function is added to expand the possibilities, with better signal there is a greater chance of finding an open, or that the process is generated successfully, without leaving aside the performance of the computer or device, so you can carry out the hacking without problems.

- **Preference persists over Linux**

Although there are programs and tools for Windows that allow hacking WiFi networks, it is best to use Linux, it is not necessary to change the operating system, but you can create a bootable CD on the computer, to use the tool from a basic aspect.

Before starting the hack process, you can incorporate a computer that is compatible with these requirements, ideally the programs should be run at their maximum capacity, otherwise even if it is the right download, it will not generate the expected effects of revealing a key or attacking a WiFi network.

- **Considers that cracking is not legal**

The practice of cracking is not entirely legal, especially when you start to generate data consumption, although it is a minor legal offense, ie you only expose yourself to a fine, plus most tools are designed to audit WiFi networks, but with its power, come to be used for a hacking goal.

- **The advantage arises over networks with lower security protocols.**

In the midst of WiFi network hacking, the focus should be squarely on networks that are of WEP type, as they provide a wide vulnerability advantage, because their own old configuration is a vulnerability that can be easily exploited.

What to do when hacking methods are used on your WiFi networks

When any of the above tools causes a breach of your WiFi security, it's time to think about strengthening every weak aspect of the network, so that access is completely contracted, immunity to hacking can be built after the following steps:

- Set the WiFi key, instead of defaulting to the router, the best solution is to customize.
- Modify the name of the network (SSID), this helps to prevent the router type from being easily known, preventing it from taking advantage of the security flaws of that brand.
- It uses WPA2 encryption, this decision or measure seeks to make it complicated or generate more time to decrypt the key by means of some software.

- Restrict the number or quantity of IP addresses, this allocation prevents the creation of hacker concurrency, another option is to place a MAC filter on the router.
- Limits the technology that is not used, this has to do with the activation of WPS.
- It has firmware that is subject to update.
- It uses an old installation, such as cable adaptation, being a much more reliable modality.

The maximum security of the WPA3 protocol

Faced with the hacking of WiFi networks, it is vital to take into account the security protocols that remain under constant innovation, as happened with the launch of the WPA3 protocol, which imposes a great concern for any purpose of attack, because the passwords are more complex to crack.

Vulnerating this kind of wireless networks is practically impossible, unless you can get an interaction with the WiFi network, and the use of old data is not feasible, as they are becoming more and more secure, at the same time, smart devices are simple to configure through WiFi Easy Connect.

Thanks to this update, even public WiFi networks become secure, all thanks to the power of its encryption, especially when looking for a specialized branch, one for domestic circles, and another for companies, although if long passwords are not used, there is still a great risk of vulnerability.

Printed in Great Britain
by Amazon